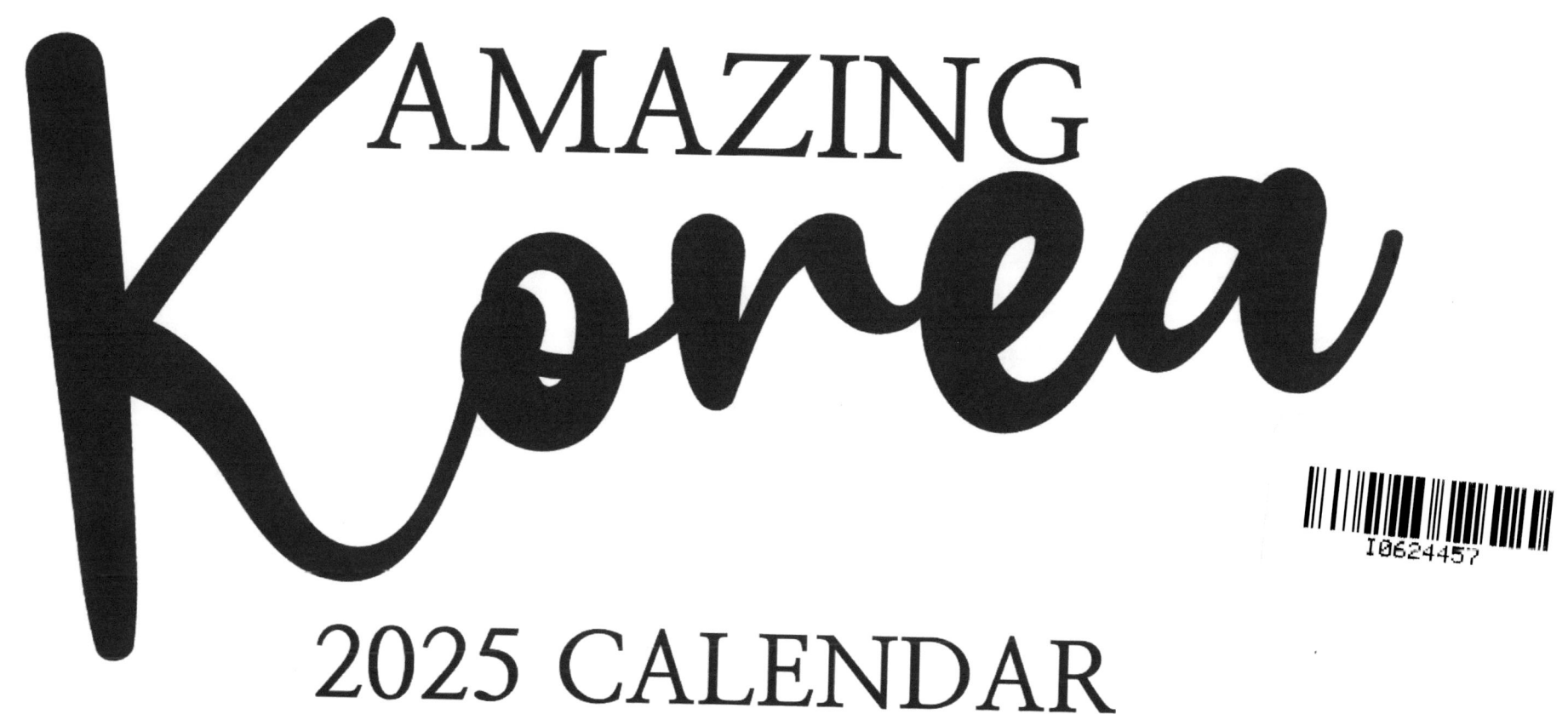

AMAZING
Korea
2025 CALENDAR

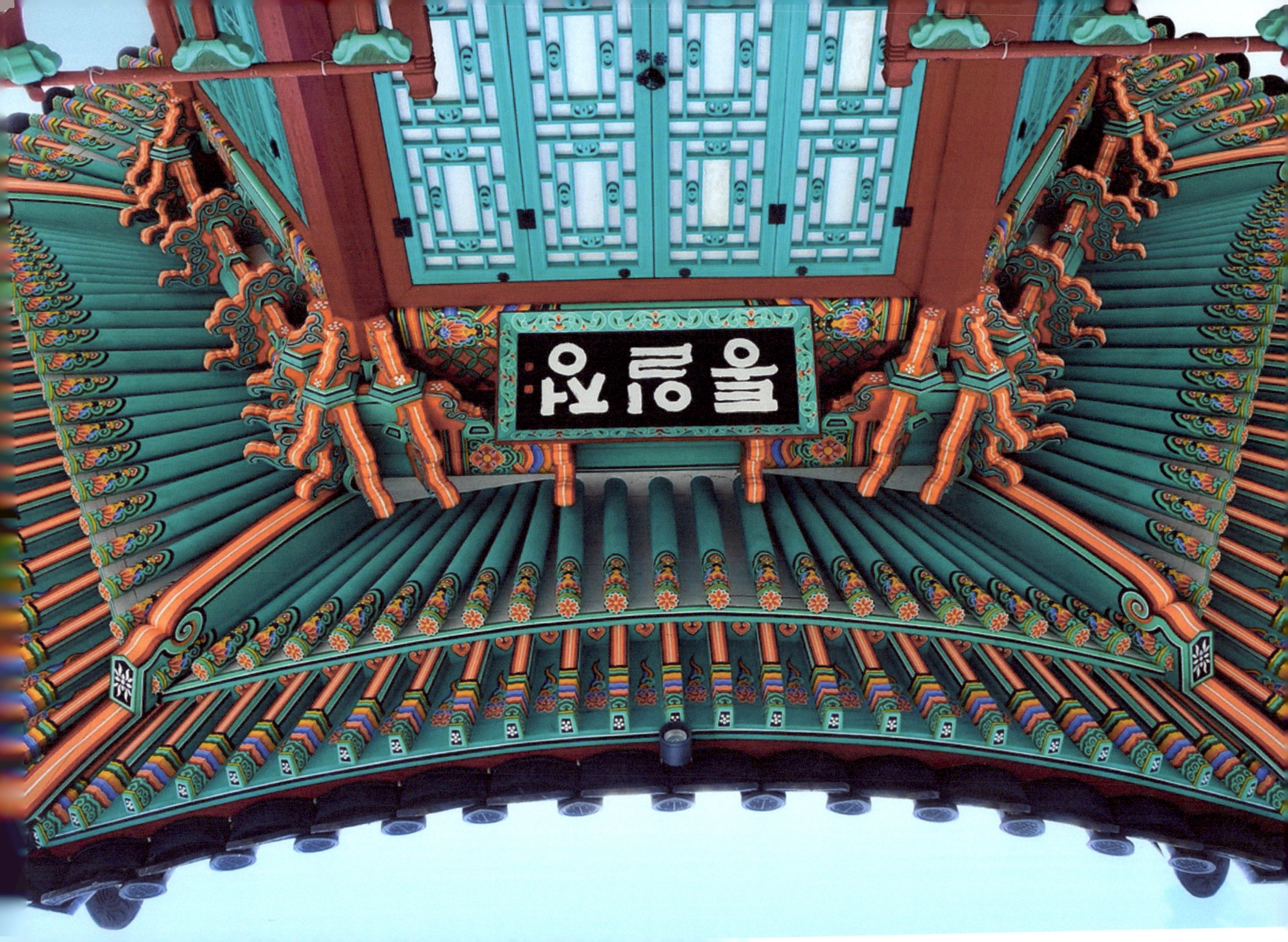

JANUARY 2025

SUNDAY	MONDAY	TUESDAY	WEDNESDAY	THURSDAY	FRIDAY	SATURDAY
29	30	31	1 NEW YEARS DAY	2	3	4
5	6	7	8	9	10	11
12	13	14	15	16	17	18
19	20	21	22	23	24	25
26	27	28 SEOLLAL (LUNAR NEW YEAR)	29	30	31	1

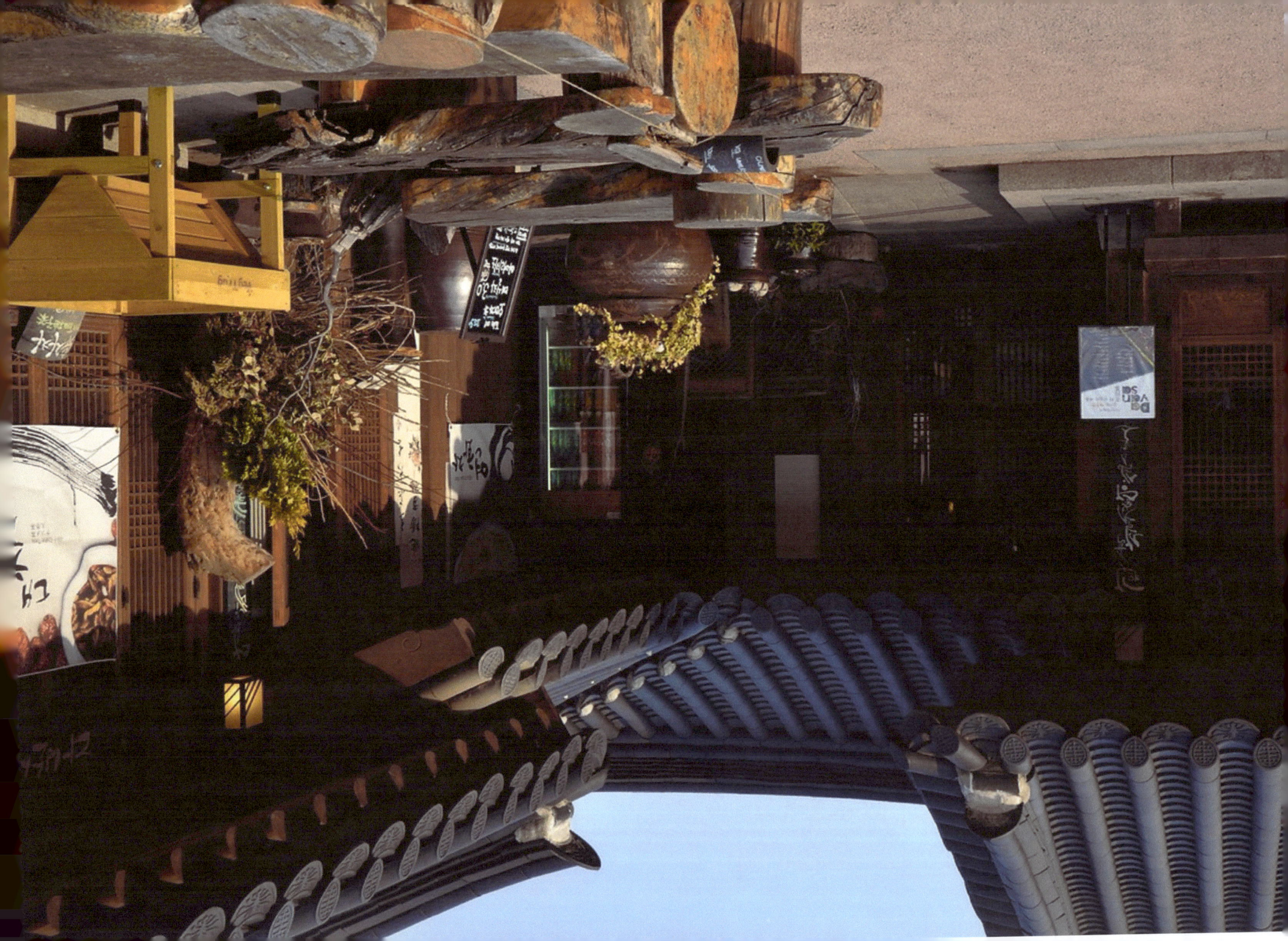

FEBRUARY 2025

SUNDAY	MONDAY	TUESDAY	WEDNESDAY	THURSDAY	FRIDAY	SATURDAY
26	27	28	29	30	31	1
2	3	4	5	6	7	8
9	10	11	12	13	14 VALENTINE'S DAY	15
16	17	18	19	20	21	22
23	24	25	26	27	28	1

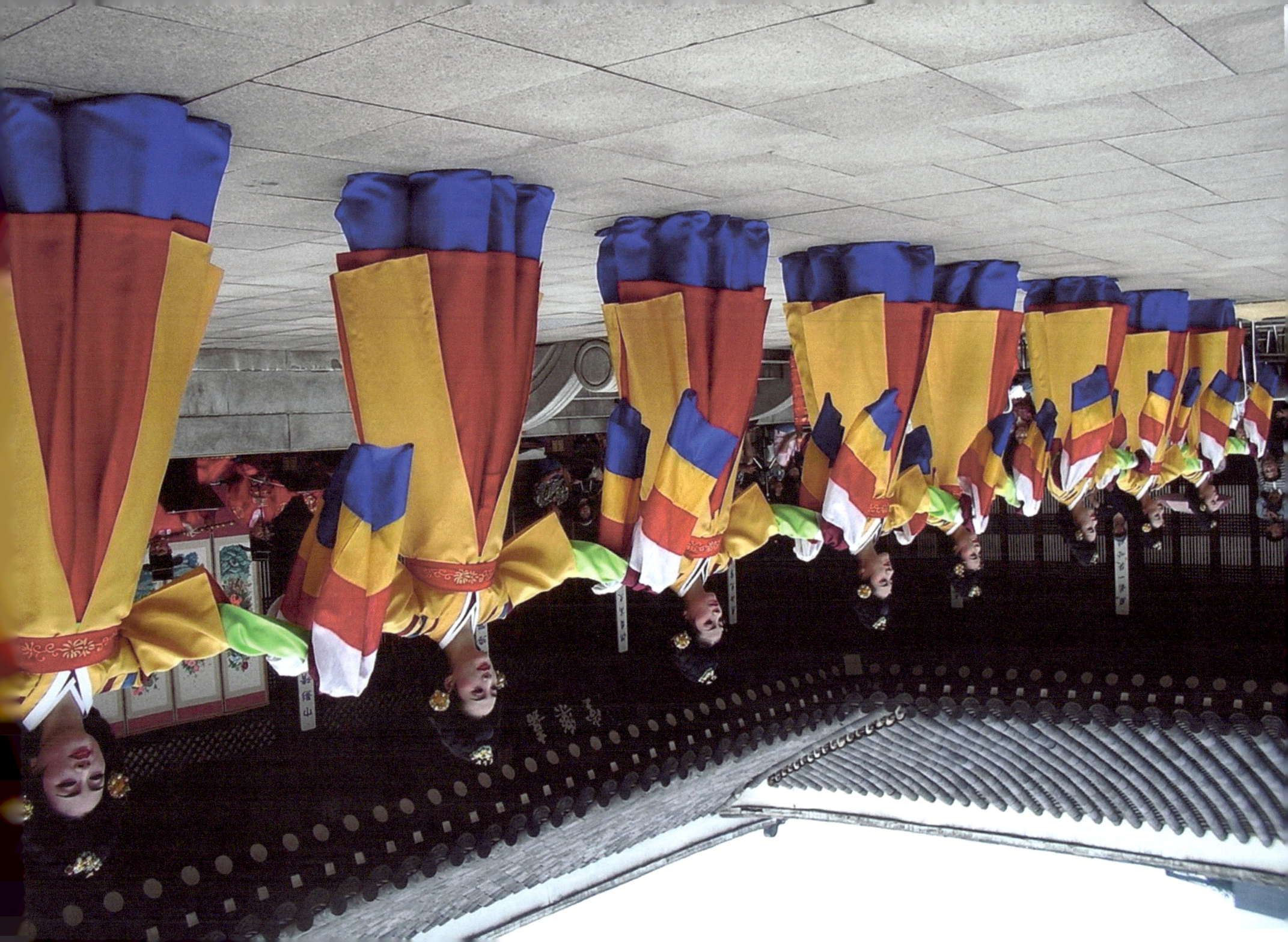

MARCH 2025

SUNDAY	MONDAY	TUESDAY	WEDNESDAY	THURSDAY	FRIDAY	SATURDAY
23	24	25	26	27	28	1 INDEPENDENCE MOVEMENT DAY
2	3	4	5	6	7	8
9	10	11	12	13	14 WHITE DAY	15
16	17	18	19	20	21	22
23 / 30	24 / 31	25	26	27	28	29

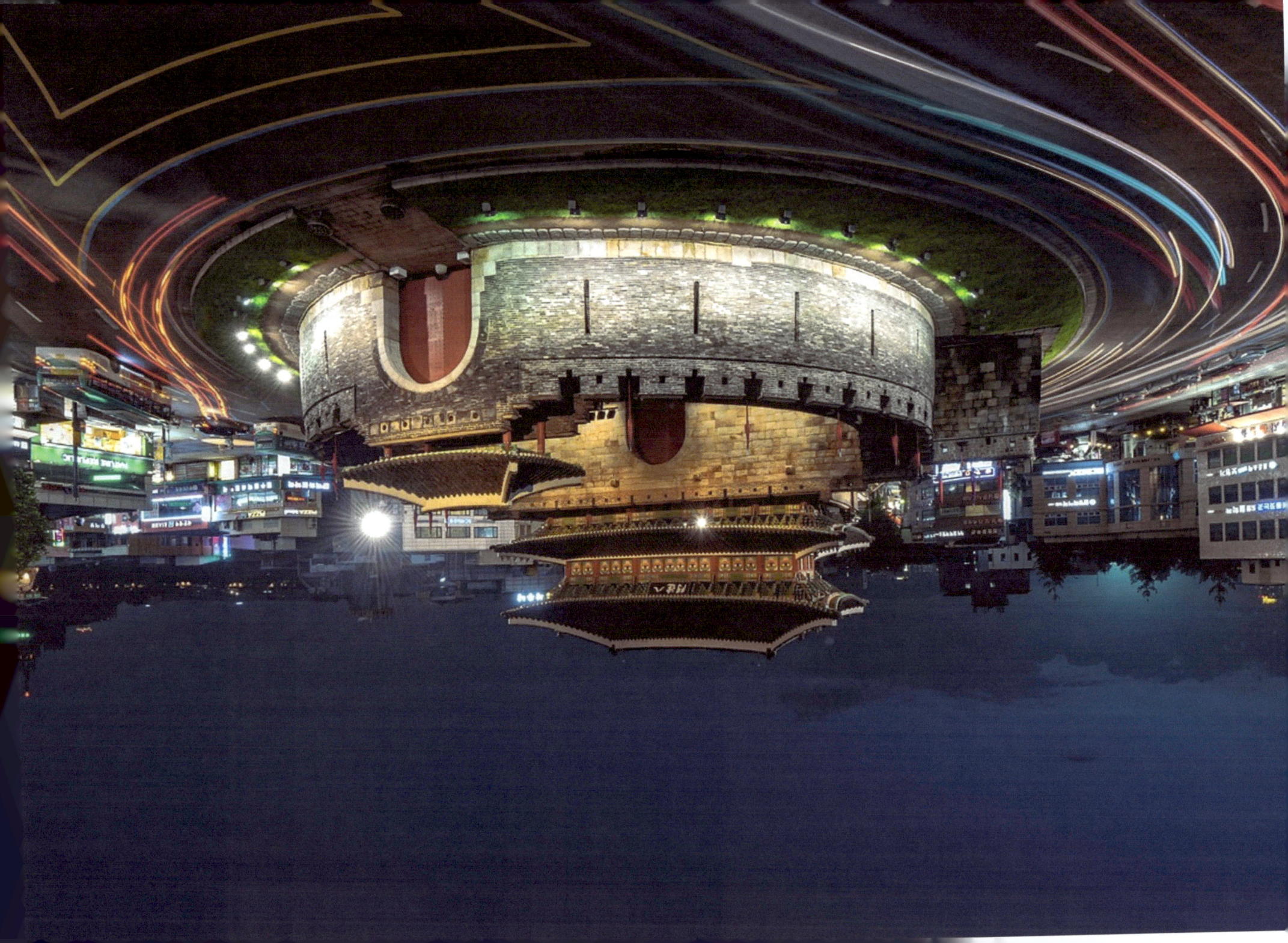

APRIL 2025

SUNDAY	MONDAY	TUESDAY	WEDNESDAY	THURSDAY	FRIDAY	SATURDAY
30	31	1	2	3	4	5
6	7	8	9	10	11	12
13	14	15	16	17	18	19
20	21	22	23	24	25	26
27	28	29	30	1	2	3

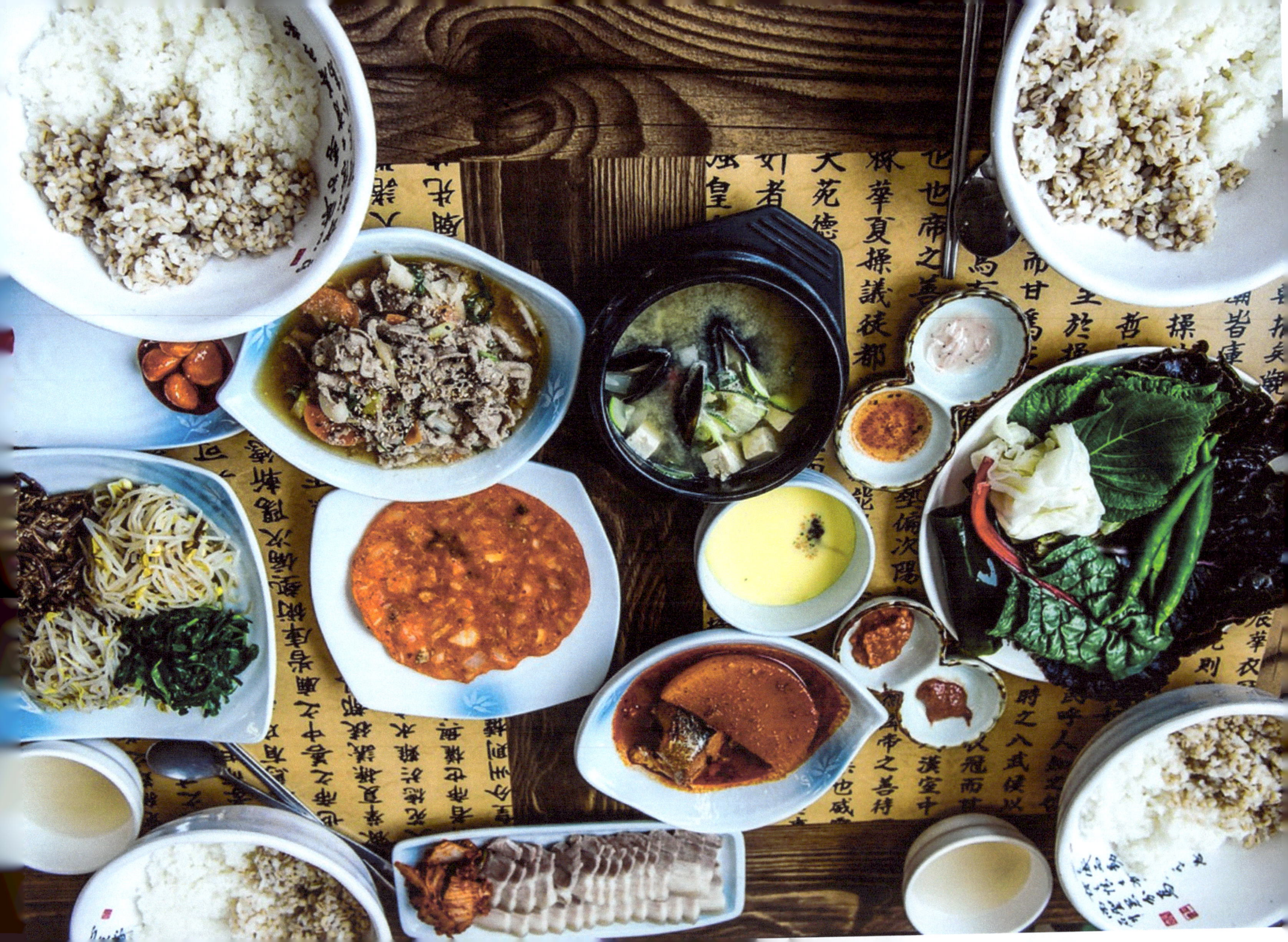

MAY 2025

SUNDAY	MONDAY	TUESDAY	WEDNESDAY	THURSDAY	FRIDAY	SATURDAY
27	28	29	30	1	2	3
4	5 CHILDREN'S DAY	6	7	8	9	10
11	12	13	14	15	16	17
18	19	20	21	22	23	24
25	26	27	28	29	30	31

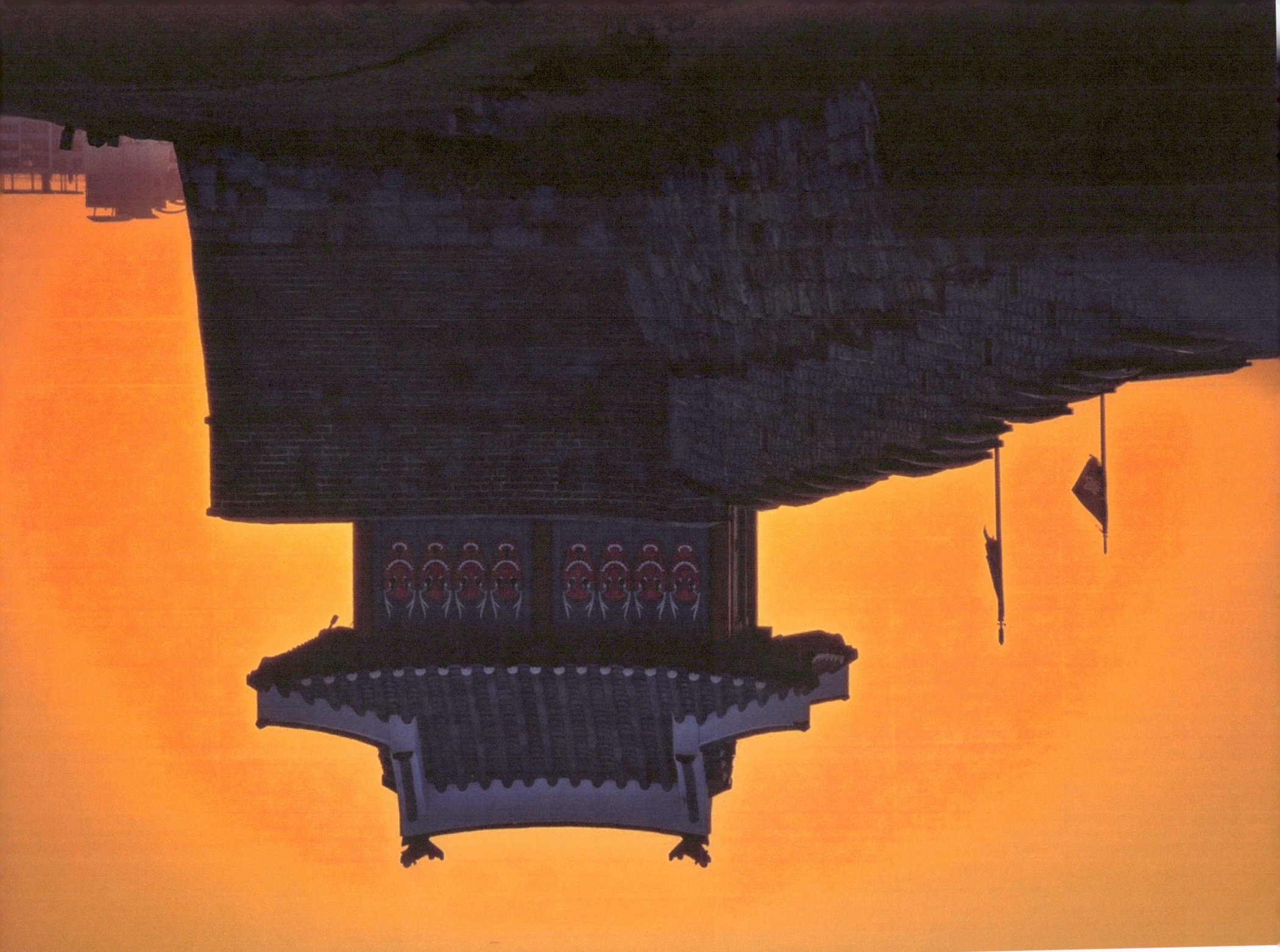

JUNE 2025

SUNDAY	MONDAY	TUESDAY	WEDNESDAY	THURSDAY	FRIDAY	SATURDAY
1	2	3	4	5	6 MEMORIAL DAY	7
8	9	10	11	12	13	14
15	16	17	18	19	20	21
22	23	24	25	26	27	28
29	30	1	2	3	4	5

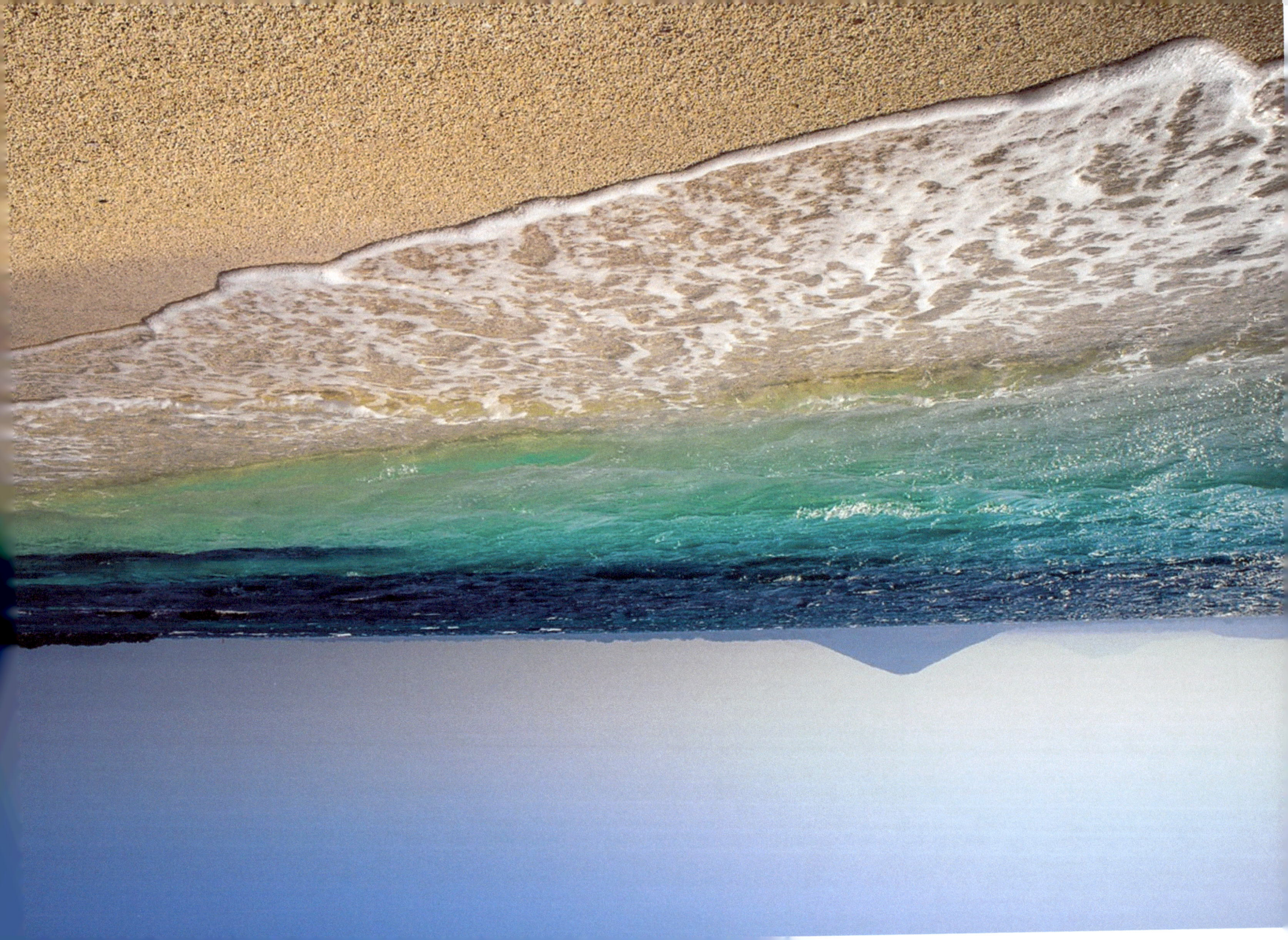

JULY 2025

SUNDAY	MONDAY	TUESDAY	WEDNESDAY	THURSDAY	FRIDAY	SATURDAY
29	30	1	2	3	4	5
6	7	8	9	10	11	12
13	14	15	16	17 CONSTITUTION DAY	18	19
20	21	22	23	24	25	26
27	28	29	30	31	1	2

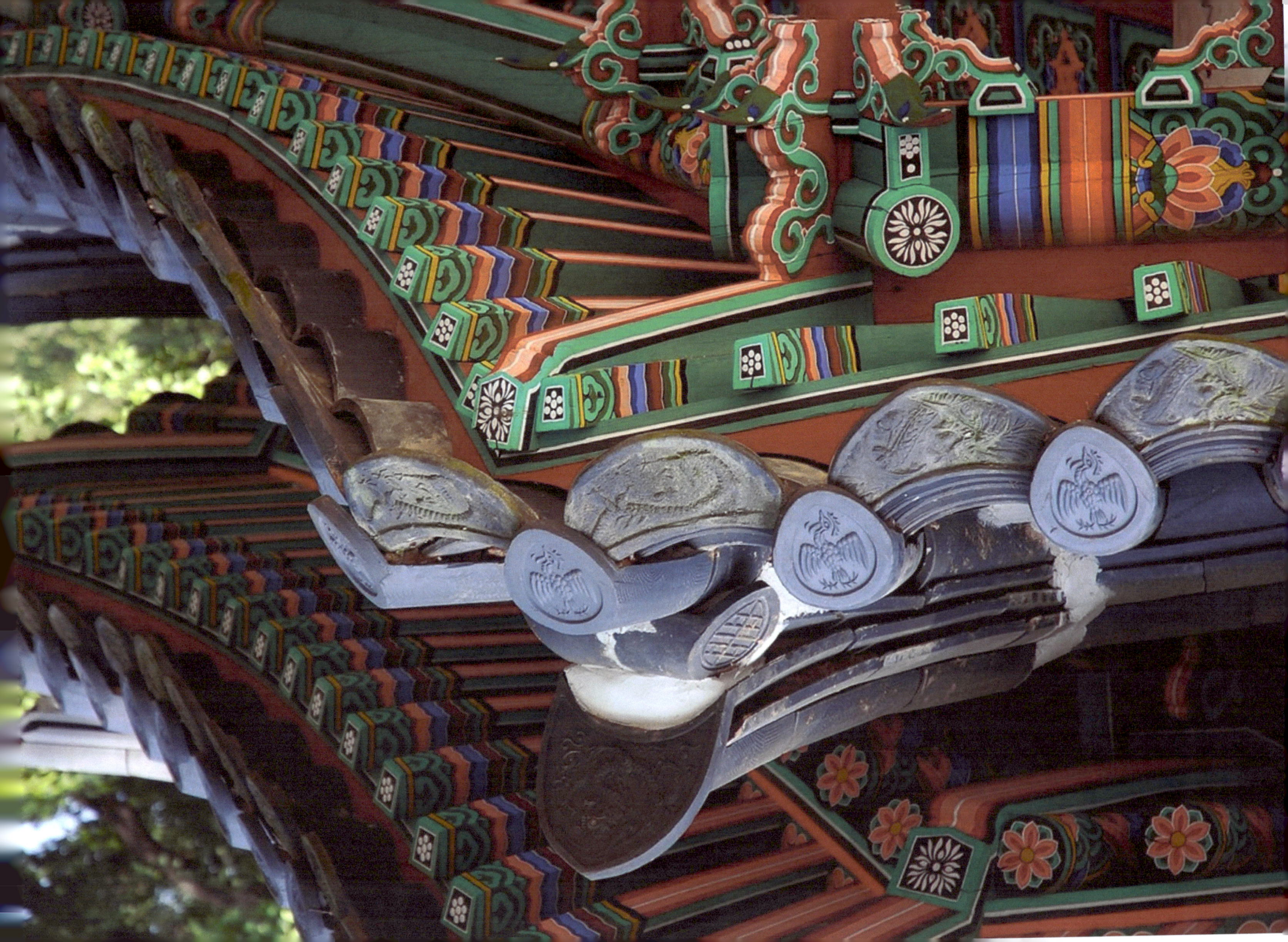

AUGUST 2025

SUNDAY	MONDAY	TUESDAY	WEDNESDAY	THURSDAY	FRIDAY	SATURDAY
27	28	29	30	31	1	2
3	4	5	6	7	8	9
10	11	12	13	14	15 LIBERATION DAY	16
17	18	19	20	21	22	23
24 / 31	25	26	27	28	29	30

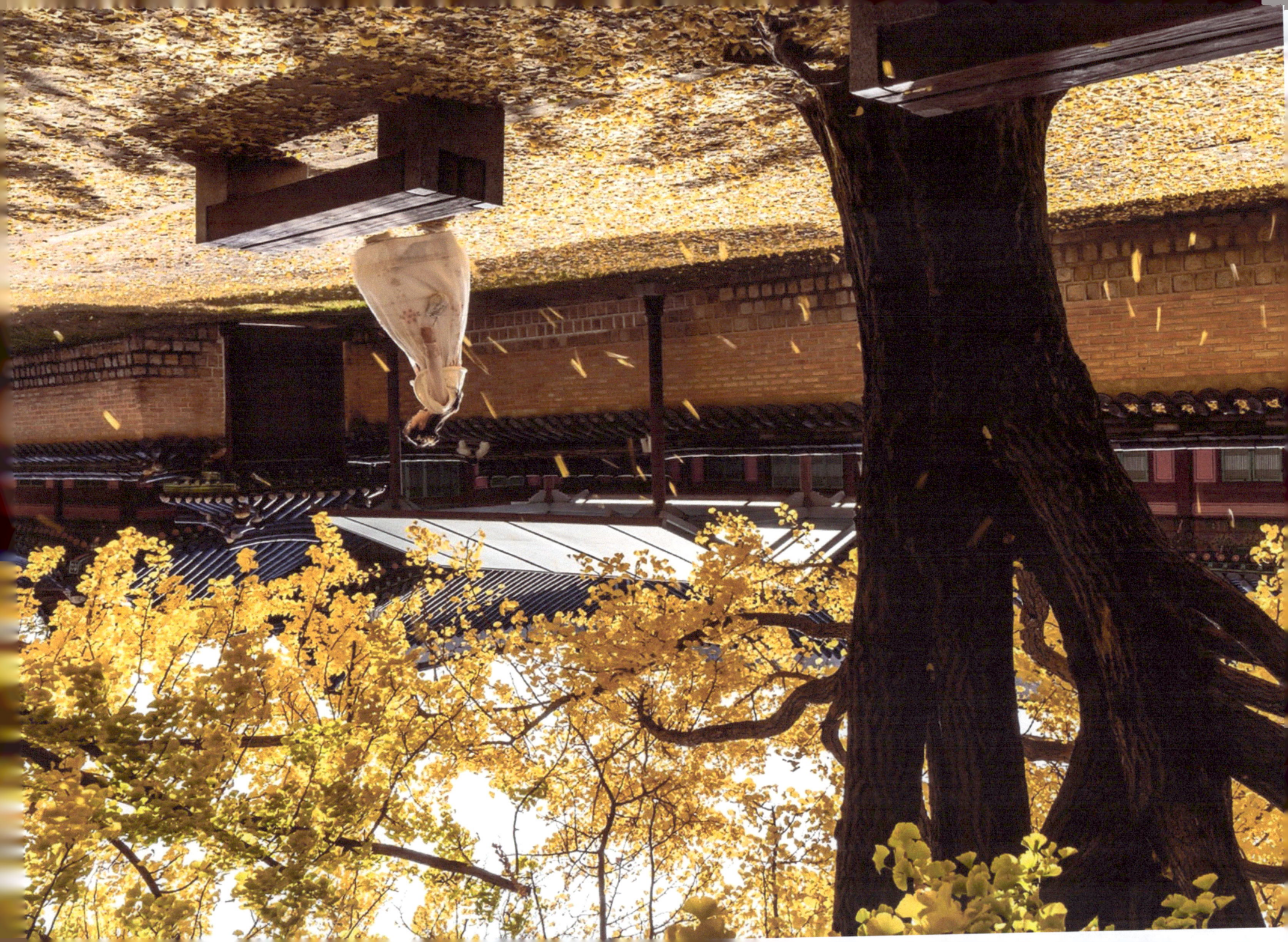

SEPTEMBER 2025

SUNDAY	MONDAY	TUESDAY	WEDNESDAY	THURSDAY	FRIDAY	SATURDAY
31	1	2	3	4	5	6
7	8	9	10	11	12	13
14	15	16	17	18	19	20
21	22	23	24	25	26	27
28	29	30	1	2	3	4

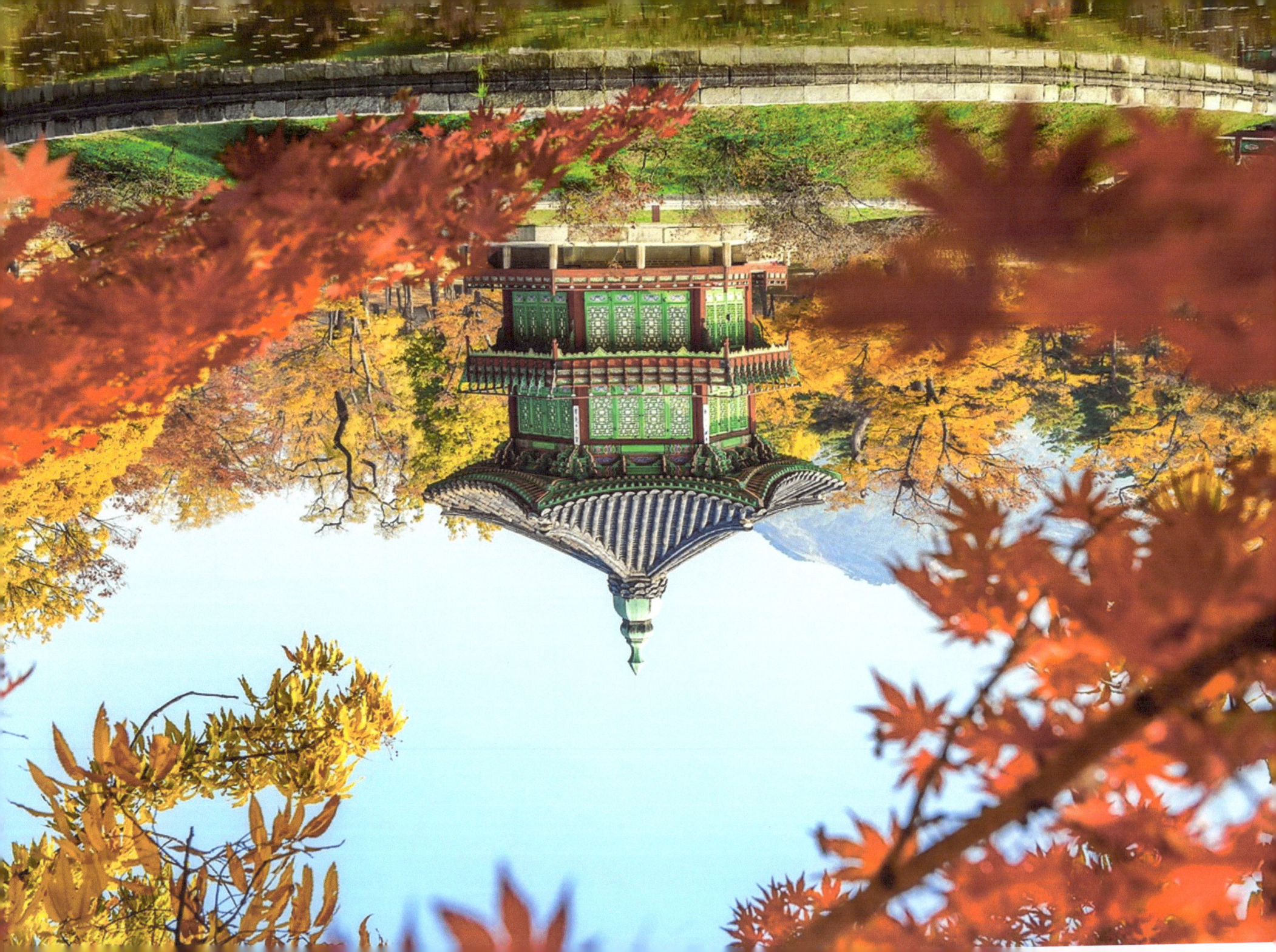

OCTOBER 2025

SUNDAY	MONDAY	TUESDAY	WEDNESDAY	THURSDAY	FRIDAY	SATURDAY
28	29	30	1	2	3 NATIONAL FOUNDATION DAY	4
5 CHUSEOK (KOREAN THANKSGIVING)	6	7	8	9 HANGEUL DAY	10	11
12	13	14	15	16	17	18
19	20	21	22	23	24	25
26	27	28	29	30	31	1

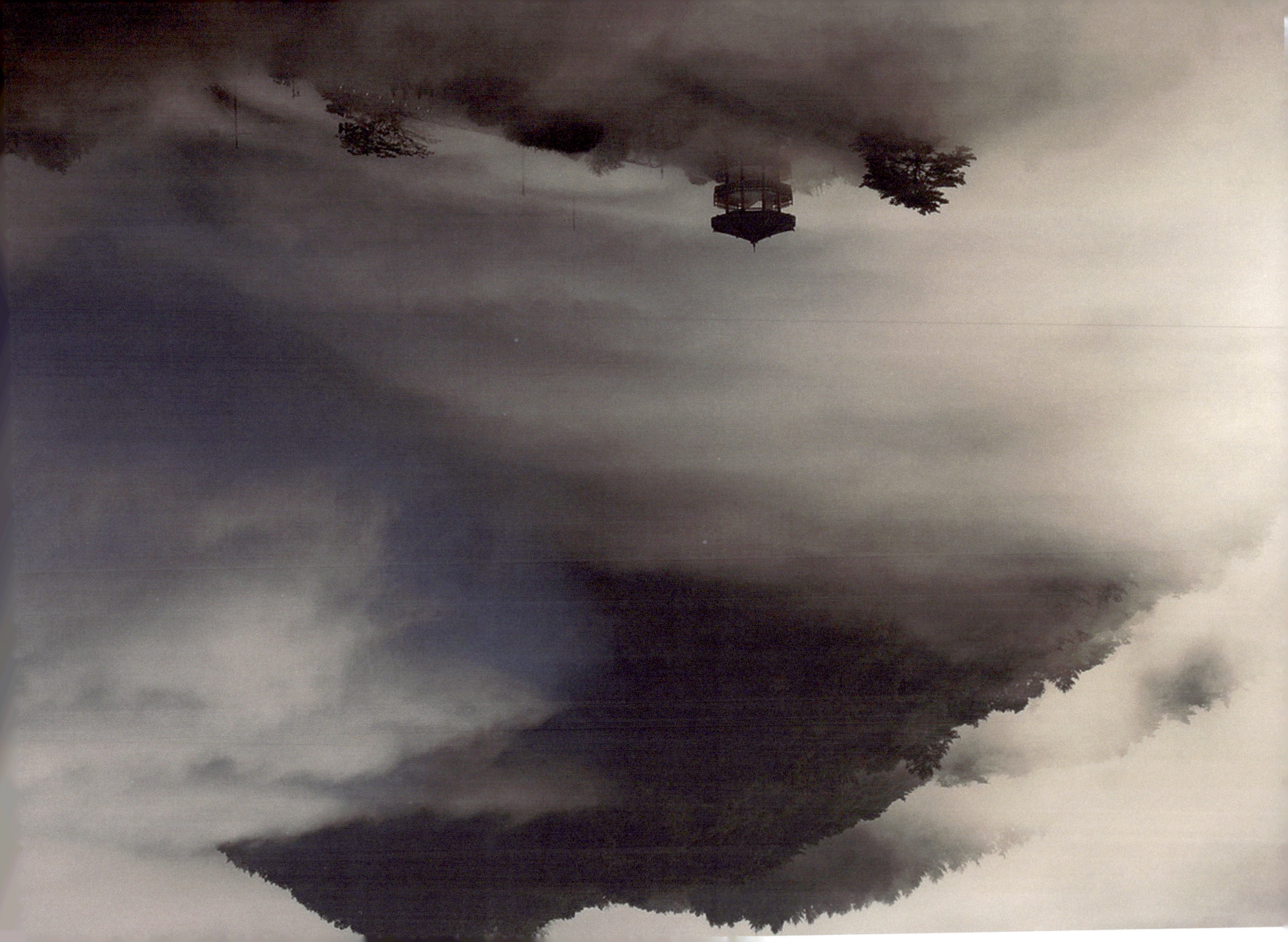

NOVEMBER 2025

SUNDAY	MONDAY	TUESDAY	WEDNESDAY	THURSDAY	FRIDAY	SATURDAY
26	27	28	29	30	31	1
2	3	4	5	6	7	8
9	10	11	12	13	14	15
16	17	18	19	20	21	22
23 / 30	24	25	26	27	28	29

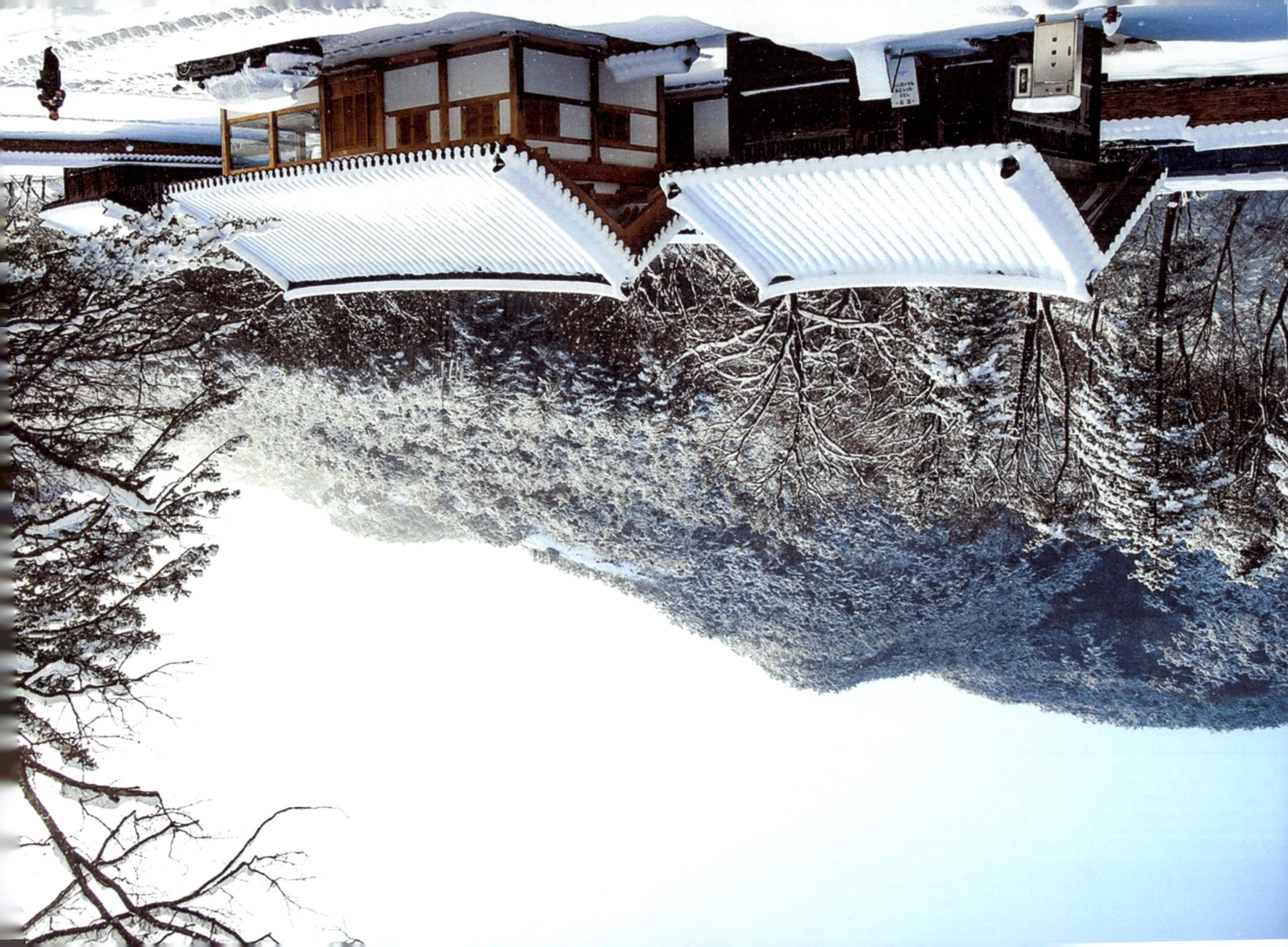

DECEMBER 2025

SUNDAY	MONDAY	TUESDAY	WEDNESDAY	THURSDAY	FRIDAY	SATURDAY
30	1	2	3	4	5	6
7	8	9	10	11	12	13
14	15	16	17	18	19	20
21	22	23	24	25 CHRISTMAS DAY	26	27
28	29	30	31	1	2	3

Korean Holidays

New Year's Day (신정) – January 1
A global holiday celebrated in South Korea, marking the first day of the year.

Seollal (Lunar New Year) (설날) – 1st day of the lunar calendar (usually January or February)
One of the most significant holidays in Korea, with celebrations lasting for 3 days. It marks the Lunar New Year, and families gather to pay respect to their ancestors and engage in traditional games.

Independence Movement Day (삼일절) – March 1
Commemorates the March 1st Movement of 1919, a key moment in Korea's struggle for independence from Japanese rule.

Children's Day (어린이날) – May 5
A day to celebrate and honor children with special activities and events for families.

Buddha's Birthday (부처님 오신 날) – 8th day of the 4th lunar month (usually April or May)
Celebrated by Buddhists in Korea, it includes temple visits and the lighting of lanterns.

Memorial Day (현충일) – June 6
A day of remembrance for soldiers and civilians who died during the Korean War and other conflicts.

Constitution Day (제헌절) – July 17
Marks the promulgation of the Constitution of the Republic of Korea in 1948.

Liberation Day (광복절) – August 15
Celebrates Korea's liberation from Japanese rule in 1945 at the end of World War II.

Chuseok (Korean Thanksgiving Day) (추석) – 15th day of the 8th lunar month (usually September or October)
One of the most important holidays, it is a harvest festival where families gather to share food, perform ancestral rites, and celebrate the season.

National Foundation Day (개천절) – October 3
Commemorates the founding of the ancient Korean state of Gojoseon in 2333 B.C. by the legendary Dangun.

Hangeul Day (한글날) – October 9
Celebrates the creation of the Korean alphabet (Hangeul) by King Sejong the Great in 1443.

Christmas Day (성탄절) – December 25
A Christian holiday that celebrates the birth of Jesus Christ, and it is also widely observed as a public holiday in South Korea.

Other Notable Observances

Valentine's Day (밸런타인데이) – February 14 (Non-official holiday, but widely observed with gift exchanges).

White Day (화이트데이) – March 14 (Similar to Valentine's Day, where men reciprocate the gifts).

Hangeul (Korean Alphabet)

Vowels (모음)

Hangul	Sound (Romanization)	Example Sound
ㅏ	a	Like "a" in "father"
ㅐ	ae	Like "a" in "bat"
ㅑ	ya	Like "ya" in "yarn"
ㅒ	yae	Like "ya" + "a" in "bat" (yae)
ㅓ	eo	Like "u" in "fun" or "o" in "son"
ㅔ	e	Like "e" in "bet"
ㅕ	yeo	Like "yo" in "yolk" (but short)
ㅖ	ye	Like "ye" in "yes"
ㅗ	o	Like "o" in "so"
ㅘ	wa	Like "wa" in "water"
ㅙ	wae	Like "wa" + "e" in "bet"
ㅚ	oe	Like "we" in "wet"
ㅛ	yo	Like "yo" in "yoga"
ㅜ	u	Like "oo" in "moon"
ㅝ	wo	Like "wo" in "wonder"
ㅞ	we	Like "we" in "west"
ㅟ	wi	Like "we" in "week"
ㅠ	yu	Like "yu" in "you"
ㅡ	eu	Like "u" in "put" or "oo" in "foot"
ㅢ	ui	Like "oo" + "ee" in "gooey"
ㅣ	i	Like "ee" in "see"

↓

Consonants (자음)

Hangul	Sound (Romanization)	Example Sound
ㄱ	g/k	Like "g" in "go" or "k" in "kite" (softer)
ㄴ	n	Like "n" in "no"
ㄷ	d/t	Like "d" in "dog" or "t" in "top" (softer)
ㄹ	r/l	Like "r" in "run" or "l" in "love"
ㅁ	m	Like "m" in "mother"
ㅂ	b/p	Like "b" in "boy" or "p" in "pen" (softer)
ㅅ	s	Like "s" in "sit"
ㅇ	silent/ng	Silent at the beginning of a syllable, like "ng" in "song" at the end of a syllable
ㅈ	j	Like "j" in "jump"
ㅊ	ch	Like "ch" in "chop"
ㅋ	k	Like "k" in "kite" (stronger)
ㅌ	t	Like "t" in "top" (stronger)
ㅍ	p	Like "p" in "pen" (stronger)
ㅎ	h	Like "h" in "hat"

Double Consonants (쌍자음) (These sounds are tense versions of their counterparts)

Hangul	Sound (Romanization)	Example Sound
ㄲ	kk	Like "g" in "go" (tense)
ㄸ	tt	Like "d" in "dog" (tense)
ㅃ	pp	Like "b" in "boy" (tense)
ㅆ	ss	Like "s" in "sun" (tense)
ㅉ	jj	Like "j" in "jump" (tense)